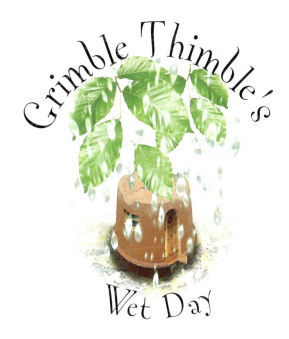

Grimble Thimble's Wet Day

Author: Ruth Stoker
Technical and Literacy Editor: Jacqui Møller-Butcher
Managing Editor: Allen Embley

Illustrations: Christopher Reading
Typography: Amanda McCormick

www.grimblethimble.org

First published in the United Kingdom
by AEP 2007. Copyright A. Embley 2007

Introducing Grimble Thimble, such a funny little man!

Grimble Thimble? Grimble Thimble!
His magic thumb is all-a-tremble…
A secret pocket? Magic dust!
A tiny man whom the fairies trust…

Grimble Thimble is a funny little man, not much bigger than the average thumb. He has a shiny brown face, bright blue eyes and curly brown hair. He has a little green jacket, made from tightly woven blades of grass. Inside this little green jacket is a tiny pocket.

Shhh! Don't tell anyone; it's a secret!

His little trousers are all shades of brown and are made from shredded autumn leaves. But he is most proud of his tiny black and white shoes. Can you guess what Grimble Thimble used to make them?

Sometimes Grimble Thimble likes to dress up. When a friend holds a garden party, he changes his little brown trousers for a pair in bright purple. To make these special, sparkly trousers, he used fairy flowers, lavender seeds and a generous sprinkling of magic silver dust.

Grimble Thimble lives in a warm, cosy flowerpot, under an old beech hedge near the bottom of a wild and wonderful garden. It was in this very garden that Grimble Thimble once fell over an old thimble. He tried it on, thinking it would make a rather nice hat, and so he gained his remarkable name: Grimble Thimble.

The garden belongs to two brave children, Abby and Jay, who love games and adventures. They met their funny little friend while searching for frogs, turning over leaves, stones and flowerpots. Can you guess where they found him? Now they are his very best buddies.

The children thought Grimble Thimble's hat looked so funny that they brought him other thimbles from their house. He now has a dainty silver one, which Abby likes best, one with a tiny rose painted on it, and a shiny purple plastic one, which he saves for special parties. The children's parents often wonder where all the thimbles have gone when they need to sew on a button!

Grimble Thimble has many garden friends: Linda Ladybird, Claude the Spider, Bertie the Blackbird and, of course, his fabulous fairy friends who live amongst the branches of the magical silver birch trees which tower over the garden, their tops lost in the clouds. Grimble Thimble is a wonderful friend. In return for his many favours, the fairies sometimes put a tiny pouch of magic silver dust in his secret jacket pocket; this magic dust makes his purple party trousers sparkle, helps him to help others and takes him on very special adventures…

Chapter One (1)
"Plop" went the raindrops

Usually, Grimble Thimble's home was warm and cosy, but this particular morning it was getting wetter and wetter. A crack had appeared in his flowerpot ceiling, and it was letting in a slow drip, drip, drip of raindrops. The raindrops grew fatter and fatter as they squeezed through the tiny gap. Each drop fell with a 'plop', splashing Grimble Thimble's hat, his table and his carpet.

The drops seemed to wink and blink in a chink of light coming through the open front door. "That 'plop' is a very cheeky 'plop', a very cheeky 'plop' indeed," Grimble Thimble grumbled aloud.

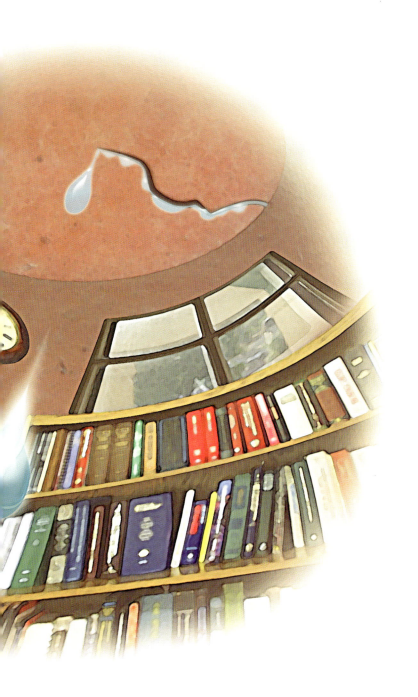

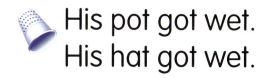 His pot got wet.
His hat got wet.

A crack let the rain
in. The rain made
his carpet wet and
made him sad.

Large drops of rain
squeezed through the
crack making his house
very wet. All the cold
water made him sigh.

Chapter Two (2)
A thimble to catch the raindrops

Grimble Thimble waited for a magic trembling in his thumb.
He couldn't feel anything at all. Not a pin, not a needle!
He would have to solve his problem without magic today.
So, the little man pushed and pulled and hauled and heaved until his
table was positioned directly beneath the crack. Can you tell what
Grimble Thimble used for a kitchen table? He used an old broken
cotton reel which still had some purple thread wrapped round it
– very handy for making party clothes! He turned his dainty
silver thimble upside down and placed it on top of the table to
collect the drips. What a good idea! "That will stop those
cheeky rain drops for now," Grimble Thimble mumbled to himself.

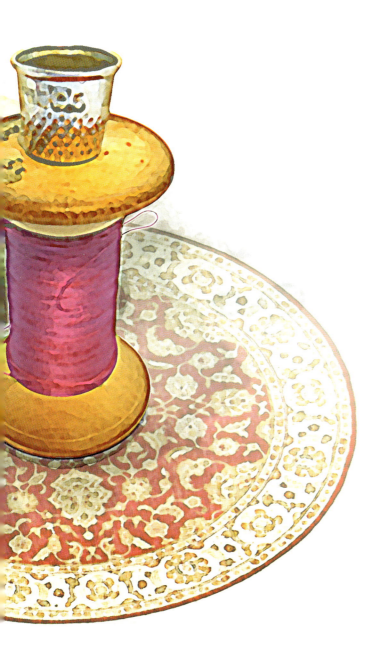

 He put up a pot.
It held the drops.

 He put a pot on his table. It held the drops of water.

 He pushed his table under the drips. He used a thimble to catch the drops. How clever!

Chapter Three (3)
Trudging across a soggy lawn

Clutching a fat, purple sage leaf that he often used for an umbrella and grumbling and mumbling all the while, Grimble Thimble went outside into the garden. He scowled at the sky, which was grey and laden with rain. He trudged across the soggy lawn, through the daisies, around the dandelions and towards the nearest flower bed. He hoped to find a suitable stone to place over the crack in his roof. Passing gingerly under the prickly branches of a dripping rose bush, a clear voice stopped him in his tracks.

"What's the matter? Why are you grumbling, Grimble Thimble?"

Grimble Thimble looked up to see the very lovely Linda Ladybird, looking most concerned – and, he thought, looking especially pretty!

 He met Linda Ladybird in the rain.

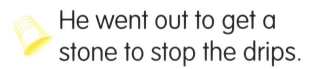 He went out to get a stone to stop the drips.

He went outside and he looked for a stone to plug the crack. Linda Ladybird looked lovely.

Chapter Four (4)
Linda Ladybird's scarlet wing cases shine

Grimble Thimble admired Linda Ladybird. Politely, he said, "I don't like the rain. Rain drops are leaking through a crack in my flowerpot roof. They have splashed my hat, my table and my carpet. I'm worried that my books will be ruined by now."

"I am sorry about your home and your books," Linda replied, "but I like the rain. It makes my scarlet wing cases shine beautifully - like magic! When it rains, I know where to catch the greenfly. They all hide together under leaves, making dinnertime very easy for me."

Grimble Thimble gave her a half-hearted smile. "It's true, your wings do look lovely," he said, "but my books really will be spoilt if I don't hurry."

Linda smiled back at him, "Goodbye, Grimble Thimble!"
With a flutter of her wings, she was gone.

 The rain fell on Linda's red wings.

 The rain made Linda Ladybird's red wings shine. She loved the rain!

Grimble Thimble knew Linda was right about the rain but he was worried about his books.

Chapter Five (5)
"Twang" and then a cry of dismay

'I could do with some magic right now,' Grimble Thimble murmured.
He patted the secret pocket in his jacket but there was still no tingling
in his thumb. It seemed his magic fairy dust was not working today.

Climbing over dripping grass stalks, Grimble Thimble trudged
around the edge of the flowerbed, scouring the wet soil for flat
stones. Without warning, he suddenly tripped, falling
headfirst into the grass. He heard a twang and then a
cry of dismay from above his head.

"Oh là, là! Qu'est-ce-que tu as fait, Monsieur Grimble Thimble?
What 'ave you done? C'était parfait! It was ze perfect web, my
masterpiece. And you snap ze anchor thread. It is ruined.
It is ruined and I 'ave used up all ze silk in my spinnerets!"

 Grimble Thimble
fell on the web.
Claude felt sad.

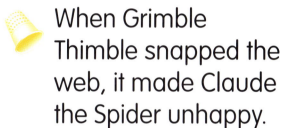 When Grimble
Thimble snapped the
web, it made Claude
the Spider unhappy.

 Grimble Thimble tripped
right over a thread of
the spider's web and
snapped it.

13

Chapter Six (6)
Claude the Spider's wonderful works of art

"I'm very sorry, Claude," Grimble Thimble said humbly. Claude the Spider was Grimble Thimble's good friend but he was also a very proud artist.

"Oh, là, là! Really! I would 'ave 'oped that in zis welcome rain you would 'ave seen my wonderful works of art and stepped over my masterpieces," Claude said.

Looking up, Grimble Thimble saw the full splendour of Claude's web. He was speechless. The rain had left glittering droplets on each thread and the whole web shone and winked at him as though it was created from tiny precious diamonds. Grimble Thimble trembled. Was it in amazement at Claude's web? No! It was his thumb. At last, his magic dust seemed to be working!

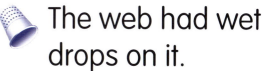 The web had wet drops on it.

Grimble Thimble saw the raindrops shine. The web looked lovely.

Claude was very proud of his pretty spider's web. The raindrops sparkled like diamonds.

15

Chapter Seven (7)
The fairy magic works at last!

Grimble Thimble patted his secret pocket. He felt sure he knew just what to do. He took the broken thread between his finger and his trembling thumb.

Claude the Spider wanted to know what Grimble Thimble was doing: "Qu'est-ce-que tu fais?" demanded Claude.

"You'll see," replied Grimble Thimble. "I've been waiting all day for this," he said softly to himself. "I can't understand why it hasn't happened before, but better late than never"

He whispered his magic rhyme:

> "I'm Grimble Thimble, Grimble Thimble!
> My magic thumb is all-a-tremble,
> My secret pocket, my magic dust!
> Helping Claude, I know I must…"

All at once, the anchor thread snapped back into place and Claude's web was perfect once more. "C'est parfait maintenant!" cried Claude happily, if a little puzzled.

Can you guess why Grimble Thimble's magic worked at that moment and not before?

 Grimble Thimble fixed the web. That made Claude glad.

 He used magic to fix Claude the Spider's web. Claude was very happy.

 His thumb trembled. He held the web and fixed it with his magic touch. Claude was delighted!

17

Chapter Eight (8)
An enormous lunch for Bertie the Blackbird

"I'm so pleased my magic worked for Claude," Grimble Thimble murmured, feeling much better. The rain had stopped and so he ambled alongside the flowerbed, still searching for a flat stone to fix his roof.

A very loud 'burrrrp' from behind made him jump and turn around to find himself face-to-feathers with Bertie the Blackbird.

"Hello Bertie," said Grimble Thimble. "You look pleased with yourself." Bertie the Blackbird grinned. The blackbird's feathers were blacker and glossier than ever while his golden beak shone brightly.

"I've just had an enormous lunch," he replied. "You see, the rain brings the worms to the surface. All I have to do is listen carefully, position myself, and then grab 'em."

"Well, I have learnt that the rain isn't such a bad thing after all. I can see it does have its uses," said Grimble Thimble.

 Bertie got worms in the rain.

 Worms came up from the ground. The rain made them come up.

The rain brought worms up out of the ground. Bertie said he caught the worms.

19

Chapter Nine (9)
The nearest stone will have to do

Grimble Thimble remembered his leaky roof. "But Bertie, my roof is still leaking and I'm worried about my books," babbled Grimble Thimble. "My silver thimble must have overflowed!"

"Don't worry," Bertie said, giving his friend a gentle pat on the back with the tip of his wing. "You'll work something out." Bertie hurriedly hopped away.

Grimble Thimble patted his secret pocket. He felt nothing. Without magic to help him, he picked up the nearest stone and trudged back through the wet grass to his flowerpot home.

He felt a little sad as he reached his front door. He felt a tingle shoot through his thumb and the wet stone slipped from his grasp, landing with a 'crunch' on Grimble Thimble's toes. He hopped up and down, mumbling and grumbling, "That's not magic! That just hurts!"

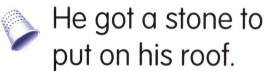 He got a stone to put on his roof.

The stone he picked up was not the right size or shape.

Grimble Thimble felt a tingle in his thumb and dropped the slippery stone right on his toes.

Chapter Ten (10)
What a lovely surprise!

"Surprise!" shouted a chorus from the flowerpot roof.

An amazed Grimble Thimble looked up to see Linda Ladybird, Claude the Spider and Bertie the Blackbird smiling down at him. They had just finished repairing the crack in his roof with "finely woven moss," according to Claude, and the perfect piece of stone: hard, flat slate which Bertie had found as he searched for worms in the rain.

At that moment, the sun appeared and shone brightly on the group of happy friends. Grimble Thimble beamed broadly and thanked everyone over and over again.

So, what is the secret to Grimble Thimble's magic? Well, his magic only works when he wants to help others!

And why did his thumb tremble just as he returned home?
Isn't it obvious? The very best kind of magic is the magic of kind-hearted friends!

 The crack in the pot had been fixed.

Linda, Claude and Bertie helped their friend Grimble Thimble. They fixed his pot.

 Grimble Thimble was delighted. His friends had fixed his leaking roof. Now that's magic!

Grimble Thimble says, "Twenty phonemes are vowel sounds. Look at how some sounds are represented by different combinations of graphemes (letters)". The sample words should clarify this.

Phoneme (the sound)	Graphemes (the different ways in which the sound can be written)			Phoneme (the sound)	Graphemes (the different ways in which the sound can be written)		
	grapheme	sample words	irregular examples		grapheme	sample words	irregular examples
/a/	a	and		/oo/	oo, u	books, put	would
/e/	e, ea	red, thread	said, many, friend	/ar/	ar, a	art, rather	are, kind-hearted
/i/	i, y	in, gym	busy, build pretty	/or/	or, aw, au, ore, al	for, lawn, hauled, before, stalks	caught, brought, your, door, broadly
/o/	o, a	on, was		/ur/	ur, er, ir, or (after w)	hurts, her, first, works	heard, journey, were
/u/	u, o, o-e	up, son, come	young, does	/ow/	ow, ou	down, outside	drought
/ai/	ai, ay, a-e	rain, dismay, make	they, eight, straight	/oi/	oi, oy	soil, boy	
/ee/	ee, ea, e, ie	green, each, he,	these, ceiling	/air/	air, are, ear	air, carefully, wear	where
/igh/	igh, ie, y, i-e, i	right, cried, my, inside, kind	height, eyes, I, goodbye, rhyme	/ear/	ear, eer, ere	clear, here, deer	pier
/oa/	oa, ow, oe, o, o-e	slow, toe, cold, stone	oh, though,	/ure/			sure
/oo/	oo, ew, ue, u-e	roof, knew, blue,	to, you, through, two, lose	/e/	Many different graphemes: silver, other, chapter, wetter, flower, fatter, under, clever, over, matter, flutter, dinner, favour, murmur, adventure, about and others		

Grimble Thimble has found some more challenging words from the story for you to read and talk about.
Look carefully at the tricky vowel sounds made by the letters underlined in each word.

Blue Thimble words the out rain he broke was made worms stone roof been

Yellow Thimble words carpet table water loved saw unhappy looked right friend

Red Thimble words lovely worried thread diamonds delighted brought said caught toe